In the Freedom of Dreams
The Story of Nelson Mandela

In the Freedom of Dreams
The Story of Nelson Mandela

Michael A. Miller

Playwrights Canada Press
Toronto • Canada

Playwrights Canada Press
The Canadian Drama Publisher
215 Spadina Avenue, Suite 230, Toronto, Ontario CANADA M5T 2C7
416-703-0013   fax 416-408-3402
orders@playwrightscanada.com • www.playwrightscanada.com

Financial support provided by the taxpayers of Canada and Ontario through the Canada Council for the Arts and the Department of Canadian Heritage through the Book Publishing Industry Development Programme, and the Ontario Arts Council.

Front cover painting of Nelson Mandela by Jeff Sprang.
Production Editor/Cover design: JLArt

Library and Archives Canada Cataloguing in Publication

Miller, Michael A.
    In the freedom of dreams : the story of Nelson Mandela / Michael A. Miller.

A play.
ISBN 0-88754-762-1

    1. Mandela, Nelson, 1918- --Drama. I. Title.

PS8626.I452515 2005   C812'.54   C2005-904168-4

First edition: July 2005.
Printed and bound by AGMV Marquis at Quebec, Canada.

I would like to dedicate this play to my father,
Clarence Allen Miller Jr.
Without him, none of this would be mine to share.

To Maxwell Sydney, Zora Cole and Charlie Rae. If they look at me with
half the love that Mandela showered on his own father,
I will be knocking on heaven's door one day.

To Iris Turcott.
You made the burden light.

To Black Fathers and their Black Sons the world over. Peace.

Introduction

A woman with no arms. This unforgettable image is one of the central metaphors in Michael Miller's play, *In the Freedom of Dreams, The Story of Nelson Mandela*. The woman, crippled by her powerful and unfeeling father, wanders lost and alone in the forest with her baby tied to her back. She cannot feed him because she is unable to reach him and her hunger, anguish and shame almost defeat her. In the end she is saved, her arms restored, and the story of how she overcomes all odds despite the cruel and unfair treatment she received becomes the stuff of legends.

Nelson Mandela is himself a living legend not only in South Africa but also around the world. When Nelson Mandela was freed from prison in February, 1990, his arms were restored to him and he was able to accomplish remarkable things for his country, his people and for humanity. Many of us have wondered how this man could emerge from prison so willing and capable to make extraordinary changes to a society that had been so cruel to him. What sustained Nelson Mandela throughout his years of incarceration in the prison on Robben Island? What experiences, influences, thoughts, and dreams influenced this remarkable man who was able to emerge from more than twenty-five years of imprisonment to skillfully (with empathy and enormous understanding) help to disarm the crippling effects of apartheid?

In the Freedom of Dreams answers some of these questions and tells the story of the young Nelson Mandela. We are introduced to his family, the people he encountered in his youth, the stories that he heard, the lessons that he learned, and the relationships and experiences that influenced him. Miller skillfully interweaves past and present, images, metaphors, voices and legends and introduces us to the story behind the hero. He deliberately makes Mandela a complex man with his own personal challenges—a man who has more difficulty being a father to his children, a son to his mother, than a leader to the African National Congress.

I celebrate the publication of Michael Miller's *In the Freedom of Dreams*. It is important that students in our schools are touched by the story of this complex, resilient, courageous and forgiving man and that they be transformed and inspired by how he lived and what he did. As teachers it is our job to "unshackle thought" and to help students express their feelings and thoughts in new and imaginative ways. This play provides teachers and students with models of language to read out loud, with complex issues of race and power to analyse, with motives of characters to interpret, with unfair circumstances of brutality to face, with metaphoric language to play with and with a complex interweaving of the play's time and place to understand. It is my hope that teachers will actively engage students in working with this text on many different levels so that they not only become more aware of Nelson Mandela's story, but that they also learn about sophisticated ways to construct and analyse a script about a difficult time and an incredible man. We owe it to our students to make our work interactive and to ask difficult questions about this script and how it is constructed so that they emerge from our classrooms more eloquent, knowledgeable and analytical.

"Dreams guide you, delude you, surprise you." This play will take students into a world where dreams of freedom become reality. It is my hope that they will emerge from that world motivated to restore the arms and voices to all people who live in unfair and brutal circumstances.

Kathleen Gould Lundy
York University
May, 2005

Playwright's Notes

Writing a play about a man who is the closest thing to a living god on earth has it's challenges. The facts of history alone can paralyse you. Add to that people's expectations and the popular mythology surrounding him and many playwrights would throw in the towel. From the beginning I knew that the play could not be just about Nelson Mandela. It had to be about the land itself. So much of who Mandela is, was tied up to his love and understanding of the land and its people. Mandela's dreams and the dreams of his countrymen, were so inextricably linked.

The hero to the world also had to become manageable and by that I mean human, and to be human is to fail and hurt others. It was through his perceived failures as a father, son, and husband that I found my entry into the humanity of this great individual. These episodes not only highlighted this man's great achievements but also helped the audience to recognise the enormous sacrifices that were made by everybody for this dearly held belief of freedom.

I also felt that to fully understand who Mandela is, you had to understand "from whence he came." The Xhosa Tribe, its customs, belief systems, stories, and social structure all informed this man's way of being, and also formed the philosophical and social bedrock for his later accomplishments. This background is what he rebelled against, and in later years is what he held dear. It's important for Western audiences to see that Mandela came from a culture that was rich in history, art, and accomplishment. We have to understand that he created his philosophy about democracy not at university but at home. This part of his experience was essential to illuminate, because it lets us see and understand the richness of this particular group of people and allows us to start seeing the complexity and sophistication that is Africa.

So I read all the facts, overcame my doubts, and tried to simply tell his/our story. Enjoy.

—MM

Production Information

In the Freedom of Dreams: The Story of Nelson Mandela was first produced at the Lorraine Kimsa Theatre for Young People in April 2003 with the following company:

Older Nelson Mandela	George Bwanika Seremba
Miss M'Dingane, Queen Victoria, Secretary, Evelyn	Nehassaiu deGannes
Chief Gadla Henry Mphakanyiswa, Walter Sisulu	Xuan Fraser
Policeman, Foreman, WM Mr. Sidelsky, Law Professor, Judge, Guard	Stephen Jennings
Buti 1 (Young Nelson Mandela), Thembi	Ngozi Paul
Buti 2 (Adult Nelson Mandela)	Andrew Moodie
Napoleon, Justice	Karim Morgan
Nosekeni, Woman	Sibongile Nene
King Jongintaba	Mxogili Welcome Ngozi

Directed by Guillermo Verdecchia
Dramaturgy by Iris Turcott
Set and Costumes by Julia Tribe
Lighting Design by Andrea Lundy
Choreography by Vivine Scarlett
Sound Design by Todd Charlton
Musical Direction by Mxogili Welcome Ngozi
Assistant Set and Costume Design by Agata Kalicki
Stage Manager: Maria Costa
Assistant Stage Manager: Michael Sinclair
Vocal Coach: Sibongile Nene

Characters

Older Nelson Mandela	Law Professor
Miss M'Dingane	Judge
Queen Victoria	Guard
Secretary	Buti 1 (Young Nelson Mandela)
Evelyn Mase	Buti 2 (Adult Nelson Mandela)
Chief Gadla Henry Mphakanyiswa	Napoleon
Walter Sisulu	Justice
Policeman	Nosekeni
Foreman	Woman
WM	King Jongintaba
Mr. Sidelsky	Thembi

Acknowledgements

The playwright would like to acknowledge the contribution and support of the entire staff of The Lorraine Kimsa Theatre for Young People. Special mention must be given to Pierre Tetrault who provided the commission and to Nancy Coy who saw the project through to completion. I'd also like to thank each member of the extraordinary cast. Special mention must be made to George and Welcome who brought such love, understanding and skill. Special thanks accorded to my favourite designer and life partner Julia Tribe who, through her design, evoked the soul of the piece. Thanks also Paul Carter Harrison who is working to see the show gets another life. To Alan MacInnes for his continued artistic support and the 2002 Play Creation Unit of CanStage.

In the Freedom of Dreams

The Story of Nelson Mandela

Act 1

Blackout. The sound of ocean. The cry of gulls. The waves lapping on shore. A night sky grows. A single light falls on NELSON Mandela. He speaks directly to the audience.

NELSON This story is not about me.

Lights up on BUTI 1.

BUTI 1 My name is Rolihlahla Madiba Mandela.

NELSON This story is not about you.

Lights up on BUTI 2.

BUTI 2 My name is Nelson Rolihlahla Madiba Mandela.

NELSON This is a story about.... Us.

Lights shift and song.

ALL Mina ngisoliwela Izwe lam
Ngizolilwel' izwelam' lizelikhuleuleke
Mina ngisoliwela Izwe lam
Ngizolilwel' izwelam' lizelikhuleuleke

NELSON My name is Nelson Mandela. I am an old man. But in my heart and in my dreams I am still a little boy. Buti. Who wakes each day to see the Drakensburg Mountains surrounding him.

BUTI 1 One day I am going to climb over you.

NELSON The sky a blanket at night and a roof in the day.

BUTI 1 There is no end to the valley.

NELSON I still feel the wind.

There is a choral sound at this point. NOSEKENI's voice.

NOSEKENI Buti. Buti.

The sound is repeated.

NELSON	Like the sweet caress of my mother's voice and I am home.
	Lights shift.
NOSEKENI	You have finished your chores?
BUTI 1	Yes. Finish the story.
NELSON	Nosekeni, my mother, told me stories for the heart. Stories of the spirit. They were my everyday lullabies.
NOSEKENI	There was a young girl with no arms.
BUTI 1	You told me that her father cut them off.
NELSON	Fairy tales that I felt I could touch.
NOSEKENI	The girl's father cut off her arms and left her lying in the forest to die.
NELSON	Despair.
NOSEKENI	But she was found.
NELSON	Hope.
BUTI 1	By who?
NOSEKENI	A very nice man. A very sweet man. A good man. He saw through the blood and the dirt. He picked her up. He brought her home and he married her.
NELSON	She told me stories of the Nation from the heart of the people.
BUTI 1	She was lucky.
NOSEKENI	She deserved that happiness. In this time of great joy she gave birth to a baby. A son. They were happy times. Life was sweet. But one cannot run from the setting of the sun. The father found out that his daughter was still alive and through a series of letters, sent to the husband by the father… she was turned out of her husband's house.
BUTI 1	What happened to the baby?
NOSEKENI	The girl's father made the husband believe that that child was not his.

BUTI 1   That's not fair. It was a lie.

NOSEKENI   Lost. Alone. Once again left in the forest to die. The baby tied to the mother's back. Three days they walked. Three days they did not eat. The baby had not eaten and the mother had no arms to comfort or nourish it.

NELSON   Stories of spirit and mythic places.

NOSEKENI   She was close to dying when a lake appeared before them.

NELSON   Stories of hope.

NOSEKENI   Water. Fresh clean water. She started to run. Run with all of her might. She knelt down to kiss the water, to take a sweet drink, to live and… and… and…

BUTI 1   What? And what?

NOSEKENI   Her lips could not reach the water. She had no arms to balance and take what she needed to live. Despair. Defeat. The girl could take no more. She had done nothing wrong but there she knelt feeling full of shame. She cried in frustration up to the heavens. She filled the forest with the howl of her grief.

> *A choral sound that extends itself for a brief moment. NOSEKENI is lost in the story along with BUTI 1. They listen to the music.*

BUTI 1   And then?

NOSEKENI   Her teardrops fell into the lake and the lake lit up.

> *Lights shift.*

From Black to Brown to Green to Yellow. Light from the lake filled the dying day with glory. The girl was dumbstruck at the sight of it. The lake began to bubble and gurgle. Like something or someone was trying to break free. Suddenly there was an explosion and a large majestic hawk rose up from the water. Its wings spanning the width of the lake. Its cry filling the valley. Thunder. Silence. Light. The majestic creature looked down on the girl with a great understanding in its eyes. He understood her anguish. He saw all the injustice that the world had reigned down upon her head. "Rise up my child. Rise up and look at me" the bird commanded and the young woman full of fright and weak from hunger still did as he commanded and saw the bird in all of his majesty. She grew afraid.

CHORUS   Do not be afraid. Do not be afraid. Do you know who I am?

BUTI 1   No.

NELSON   I wondered who that woman was for many years. Who my mother was talking about and then one day it hit me.

NOSEKENI   The bird opened it's wings to her and said: I am your ancestor. Come to me.

CHORUS   Come home.

NELSON   That woman was my home. South Africa.

BUTI 1   She died?

NOSEKENI   I never said she died. Remember this, Buti. The ancestors always provide.

CHORUS   *Na me baz za. (translation: The men are coming)*

              The bird rises. The bird cries. Lights shift. The two of them watch and listen to the bird.

BUTI 1   Look. *(The cry of the bird.)* Father is coming.

NELSON   When I grew up I wanted to be just like him.

              BUTI 1 bends down and rubs a white spot of dirt in his hair. Lights shift.

              He knew everything about the history of our people. All of the great Kings and Warriors. Our battles with the English and the Boers over our land.

NOSEKENI   Remind your father to come straight home.

NELSON   He was my school and my teacher.

NOSEKENI	Straight home.
	BUTI 1 runs off. Man from CHORUS stops him.
CHORUS	Where do you think you are going?
NELSON	Father's stories were filled with men fighting for what they believed in.
BUTI 1	I am going to see my father.
CHORUS	You have time for one match.
BUTI 1	I have to go and see my father.
CHORUS	I smell something.
BUTI 1	I am going to meet my father.
CHORUS	I know what it is now. That stinking smell. I know what it is now.
BUTI 1	I don't smell anything.
NELSON	I admit to a weakness.
CHORUS	I do.
BUTI 1	What does it smell like?
CHORUS	Chicken.
NELSON	I could never resist a good battle and stickfighting was my passion.
	The CHORUS makes loud chicken noises. BUTI 1 pulls out his stick.
	I loved to fight. Whenever I fought I would feel myself being filled up with the stories of these great men and their glorious deeds. The great Xhosa Kings.
	Each of the men from the CHORUS pulls out his stick and brandishes it while chanting the names of the chiefs.
CHORUS	Siyolo Xoxo Stowkwe Tembu Ndlambe

>   Ngqika
>   Hintsa.

BUTI 1   Let's fight.

>   *A battle erupts among the men. Lights shift. They are
>   boys stickfighting each other. There must be joy amongst
>   the battle. BUTI 1 knocks down his opponent. It is
>   a fierce battle.*

>   That was not chicken you were smelling. It was
>   defeat.

NELSON   I still see him coming.

>   *Lights up on CHIEF Gadla Henry Mphakanyiswa.
>   BUTI 1 beats his opponent.*

BUTI 1   I am still the champion.

NELSON   I wanted nothing more than to make him proud of
             me.

>   *The fallen boy extends his hand. BUTI 1 makes
>   a violent move towards him. He rises and smiles at his
>   father.*

BUTI 1   I am still the champion.

CHIEF   When Hintsa, the great paramount Chief of our
             people, was captured by the British, the Xhosa went
             to war to free him. While escaping from the British,
             Hintsa was shot by a soldier in the leg like a dog. Our
             King. He managed to drag himself out of the camp
             and find shelter under a rock. The soldier followed
             him to his hiding place and instead of offering him
             assistance and care as he should have done a King, he
             shot this unarmed defenseless King. The British then
             cut off his ears and placed them in a jar of alcohol as
             a souvenir of their great victory. They rubbed our faces
             in the mud of their contempt. Are you a British man
             or a Xhosa man?

BUTI 1   Xhosa...

CHIEF   Pick your friend up out of the dirt. You can defeat
             a man, my son, but you never, never, disgrace him.

You took his pride. Leave him his dignity. Act like a man. A Xhosa man. Pick him up.

> *A song. BUTI 1 is cowed by the previous words. The boy's hand is still extended. The previous tableaux is repeated. The two boys' hands meet. BUTI 1 helps him to his feet, brushes him off and holds out his hand to his opponent. Lights shift. CHIEF opens his arms up to his son. BUTI 1 runs to him.*

NELSON	He certainly was my teacher and my school.
BUTI 1	How was the King?
CHIEF	He is doing very well.
BUTI 1	What do you say to the King?
NELSON	Father was a principal advisor to the King. A great councillor.
CHIEF	You say what you truly believe. We gather together. The King has asked us to come and he is obliged to listen to what each of us has to say. I only say what I think is true. That is what every man must do. For the good of the people and the tribe. I also tell the King the stories of his ancestors to help him make a decision.
NELSON	History is a wonderful gift.
CHIEF	You must remember that the Xhosa have done great things. That we had occupied this land for twenty generations. Those mountains used to be our battleground. We fought the British through seven wars. We won six of them. Them with guns and we with our spears and our mountains. But we lost the mountains.
NELSON	He had a fierce love of the land and its people.
CHIEF	In the end we lost the mountains and we lost our advantage.
BUTI 1	We must get them back. These mountains were ours first. I hate the British.
CHIEF	You don't know anything about them.

BUTI 1	I know that they have the mountains now.
CHIEF	The ancestors will provide.
	The two men start the journey home. Song. Lights shift.
BUTI 1	Mother, I did it. I came straight home.
	NOSEKENI enters with a pair of pants.
NOSEKENI	Thank you Buti. You wanted these when you came home.
	NOSEKENI gives pants to CHIEF.
CHIEF	I have something for you. You will need to change into these for your journey.
BUTI 1	Where will I be going?
CHIEF	To learn about the British.
NOSEKENI	You are going to the British school.
BUTI 1	I don't like the British. I hate them.
CHIEF	At school you will hear their side of our story and those mountains. Once you have heard their side then you can really decide if you dislike the British. All I ask of you is that you do your best and that you be fair to your people and to the British as well.
NELSON	No gift was ever as sweet as those pants. They marked me out as a special boy. A child with a future. School was a rare and precious gift just like those pants.
BUTI 1	I promise to do my best.
NELSON	My dream was to make my father proud.
BUTI 1	When I grow up I want to be just like you.
CHIEF	Give me your sticks. You will not be needing them at school.
NOSEKENI	But you will need this smaller stick.
	BUTI 1 hands over his stick. NOSEKENI gives BUTI 1 a pencil. The lights shift. A few bars of "God Save our Gracious King" are sung. The class assembles. BUTI 1 enters and tries to find a spot.

CLASS	God save our gracious King, long live our noble King. God save our King. Send him victorious, happy and glorious, long to reign over us, God save our King. Good morning Miss M'Dingane.
M'DINGANE	Class we have a new student today. Young man. Please tell us your Christian name.
BUTI 1	My name is Rolihlahla Madiba Mandela. I am seven years old.
	The students laugh.
M'DINGANE	I asked you for your Christian name.
BUTI 1	Rolihlahla?
	The laughing increases.
M'DINGANE	I take it you don't have a Christian name then.
BUTI 1	I am sure that my father must have one for me at home.
	The students laugh.
M'DINGANE	I will give you one.
BUTI 1	But my father must…
M'DINGANE	Your father has no say in this.
BUTI 1	He is my father.
M'DINGANE	Quiet. *(silence)* You are Nelson.
BUTI 1	Who is he?
M'DINGANE	He is you.
NELSON	Each of my names had a special meaning. Each was connected to an ancestor of mine. A story of my father's.
BUTI 1	Tell me who this Nelson is?
M'DINGANE	Do you know the meaning of Rolihlahla?
BUTI 1	The puller of branches.

Beat.

Troublemaker.

> *Laughing from the CHORUS. M'DINGANE raises her hand for silence. The laughing stops.*

M'DINGANE See that you are not going to live up to that name in my class. You are Nelson Mandela. That is the name you will answer to. Is that clear Nelson Mandela?

BUTI 1 Yes Miss M'dingane.

M'DINGANE Class, please say hello to Nelson Mandela.

CHORUS Good morning Nelson Mandela.

BUTI 1 But who is he? Who have you named me after? My father is going to ask me.

M'DINGANE It is the name that I am giving you. If you want to learn about the British you must have a Christian name. Tell him that for me. Please. Now open your books to page twenty-two…

NELSON Mrs. M'dingane gave me one of my first dreams. One day I was going to find out who my English ancestor was. I was going to do that all by myself. We studied English History but nowhere did I find an English King by the name of Nelson. I studied more and more and finally one day I found him.

BUTI 1 The Story of My English Ancestor.

> *A group of African men stand in English uniform. We hear cannon fire and rifle shots. Lights up on QUEEN Victoria.*

QUEEN I come to you with a heavy heart. Napoleon has declared war on England, Lord Admiral Nelson.

> *BUTI 1 dons an English hat along with his stick. He raises his stick on NAPOLEON. Lights up on NAPOLEON.*

NAPOLEON The English alone cannot defeat the might that is France.

QUEEN Did you hear what he called the channel?

NAPOLEON	A ditch that will be crossed by the one with the audacity to do it.
QUEEN	I will not have that man in England. I am giving this country to you for safekeeping, oh great and wonderful and marvelous and heroic…

BUTI 1 kneels at the feet of the QUEEN.

NELSON	I thought a lot of myself back then. I was one of the smartest children in my class.
QUEEN	Do it for me. Do it for Britain.
BUTI 1	I would be honoured, my Queen, for the English empire represents all that is good and civilised in the world. We stand for justice. We stand for civilisation.
NELSON	I was enthralled with the story of the British and their world.
BUTI 1	I will fight for the empire and I will fight for the honour of this great nation.
QUEEN	You are a true son of England, Lord Nelson.
BUTI 1	To war. To arms.
CHORUS	You son of a gun, you won't get rich, you're in the army now You son of a gun, you won't get rich, you're in the army now You son of a gun, you won't get rich, you're in the army now You're in the army now, soldier, you, you son of a gun.

The men cheer. A full scale ships' battle ensues.

BUTI 1	We have fought them for two years at sea. Tooth and nail. On land and on sea. Defeat. Despair. Until one day. Look. There it is, men.

A full battle among the boys erupts.

Victory is within our grasp.

NELSON	For Victory.
BUTI 1	Fight on.

NELSON	You must…
BUTI 1	Fight on.
	The fight continues. Smoke. Canons. Gunshots.
	Victory is at hand.
	A gunshot. A loud yelp. Chimes, bells, singing. The QUEEN arrives. Lights shift.
QUEEN	No man has defended the empire in the manner of this great man. Let us bestow upon him our highest honours. Let songs be composed that will be sung by our children and our children's children. Let the bells ring proclaiming the might and the valour of our saviour Lord Nelson.
NELSON	Thanks Vicky.
	The men raise BUTI 1 on their shoulders.
BUTI 1	I got an A and I am still the stick-fighting champion of my village Qunu.
NELSON	What a joyous time it was in the country as a young boy.
BUTI 1	I am still the champion.
NELSON	I was so free.
BUTI 1	I can't wait to tell my father.
	NOSEKENI enters.
NELSON	But you cannot escape the setting of the sun.
NOSEKENI	He wishes to see you.
BUTI 1	He is home?
NOSEKENI	Yes.
BUTI 1	But he is not home for two more days yet.
NOSEKENI	He has come home early.
	The boys set him down. Lights up on CHIEF Gadla Henry. He is coughing.
BUTI 1	Father?

NOSEKENI	Shhhh. Go quietly Buti.

*Lights shift. Soft music. CHIEF Gadla Henry sits.
A fire burns in front of him. It is night.*

CHIEF	A good mark on your report and still the stick-fighting champion. Congratulations.
BUTI 1	And I found my English ancestor. He was a great warrior father. He died for his country.
CHIEF	Then he was great indeed. You are being fair. Thank you.
BUTI 1	So tell me about a Xhosa warrior. One of the great ones. Siyolo, Xoxo.
CHIEF	Not now. I'm very tired. Just remember one thing, my son. Always be fair.
BUTI 1	Will you tell me tomorrow about a Xhosa warrior?
CHIEF	Tomorrow? *(beat)* I hope so. Goodnight, my son.
BUTI 1	Goodnight Father.

*Lights shift. A song. NOSEKENI enters. She grabs
NELSON and hugs him.*

CHORUS	Iyo baphe abantu. Hisifo esibi. Hisifo segazi.
Iyo baphe abantu. Hisifo esibi. Hisifo segazi.
Iyo baphe abantu. Hisifo esibi. Hisifo segazi.

Repeats until body of CHIEF Gadla Henry is removed.

NELSON	My father died in the night.

A repeat of the King's chant.

CHORUS	Siyolo
Xoxo
Stowkwe
Tembu
Ndlambe
Ngqika
Hintsa
Gadla Henry
Gadla Henry

BUTI 1	My father has died.
NELSON	The great bull. My teacher. My school. Gone. The world was changing before my very eyes. The world I knew and that I understood was lost to me. Where would we live now? How would we eat? Who would pay for the food? Who would pay the rent on the land? Who did we pay the rent to? Was this even our land? As the eldest son in my mother's house, I was now the man of the house.
BUTI 1	The Great Bull is dead.
NELSON	I was nine years old.
	BUTI 1 gives the pencil back to NOSEKENI.
BUTI 1	I won't be needing this pencil anymore.
NELSON	Father was the mountains that surrounded me. He was the valley and the sky. The land all around me. The mountains that we had lost.
BUTI 1	I keep wanting to run to the road and see if Father is coming home.... Mother we don't have anything.
NOSEKENI	Your father left something for you and we have to go and get it. We are going on a trip.
BUTI 1	A trip where?
NOSEKENI	Over the mountains.
NELSON	I was spirit.
BUTI 1	I want to beat the sun.
NELSON	There was light in the night sky.
BUTI 1	A trip? Father left something for me? Come on Mother. We must go and get it. Race you there.
NELSON	A new dream cracked open.
BUTI 1	I finally get to climb the mountain.
NELSON	Guess what I saw when I went to the top of the mountain?
BUTI 1	There are mountains for miles and miles.

NELSON	More mountains.
BUTI 1	One day I am going to climb every one of you.
NOSEKENI	Look back my son. Look back.
NELSON	I regret that I never did what she told me to do that day.

The scene shifts during the action of the song. We are in the court of KING Jongintaba. The village of Mqhekwezeni.

A song of greeting for the King is sung.

WOMEN	Ngubani na lo Os'bizel' endundleni
MEN	Ngujongintaba ingonyama yesizwe
WOMEN	Ngubani na lo Os'bizel' endundleni
MEN	Ngujongintaba ingonyama yesizwe
NOSEKENI	Bow your head.

KING Jongintaba appears.

NELSON	What a day that was. To see the King of our nation coming towards me. Jongintaba. His name means "One who looks at the Mountain." And he had his eyes on me.

Song ends.

KING	Sweet Sister. We share your loss. The whole tribe shares in your grief.
NOSEKENI	And it makes my burden so much lighter to bear. I thank you my King.
NELSON	The King. Jongintaba.
KING	You have brought the boy.
NOSEKENI	As his father requested.
NELSON	What was this about?
KING	Look at me Madiba. Your father made one last request to me before he died and I said that I would see that it got done. He said that you were a very smart young

	man with promise. He thought that you would serve the tribe well in the future. He said you were never a problem and obeyed him. He said you were a wonderful son.
NELSON	I wanted to go home. I was scared. My clothes were dirty. My feet were dirty and I was standing before the King and his court.
KING	Your father asked that you be a servant in my house until you become a man.
NELSON	He wanted me to live here? Light.

The crowd responds favourably to this information.

NOSEKENI	Thank you, my King. It would be a wonderful honour for him to serve you and his people.
KING	I am not granting his request.
NELSON	I started to fall. I had to go home. No.
KING	Your father was a great man and his son deserves more than to be a servant. I have no need of any servants, Madiba, but I would like to make you my son.
CHORUS	*Bayete.*
KING	You will be raised in the house of the King.
NELSON	I was going to eat what the King ate.
KING	Wear what the prince wears.
NELSON	I could finish school and go on to university. My dream.
KING	And in return for this, my son, all that I ask, is that once you become a man, take up your place as counsellor to my son, Justice, who will take my place once I am gone. Justice. This is your new brother. Rolihlahla Nelson Madiba Mandela. Show him the grounds.

At this juncture the KING speaks in the Xhosa to the CHORUS who depart.

JUSTICE	Are you going to stand there looking at nothing or come with me?
	BUTI 1 raises his head. He walks toward JUSTICE. JUSTICE looks him up and down.
NELSON	I could not speak.
JUSTICE	Come on let's go.
	Lights shift. The court fades. A fence is seen in the distance.
	You don't say much do you?
NELSON	My eyes were hungry, just taking it all in.
JUSTICE	Your face is twisted up like an old man's. I think that is what I'll call you, Old Man.
BUTI 1	I am not an old man.
JUSTICE	You act like one with that serious face.
BUTI 1	Father has a beautiful bull in the krall.
JUSTICE	It's Father's prize bull. The White farmer on the next farm is always asking Father to sell it. The bull makes more noise than you do.
BUTI 1	You have a very nice home.
JUSTICE	It's *our* home now, or weren't you paying attention, Old Man?
BUTI 1	Please don't call me that name.
JUSTICE	What name.
BUTI 1	That name.
JUSTICE	Old Man?
BUTI 1	I counted fifty head of cattle.
JUSTICE	Only old men count cattle.
BUTI 1	There are hundreds of sheep.
JUSTICE	Five hundred.
BUTI 1	Five hundred sheep.

NELSON	That was a fortune. Justice was a boy of the world.
JUSTICE	Come on. Let's go home.
BUTI 1	Have I done something to make you mad?
JUSTICE	Do you dance?
BUTI 1	Not very…
JUSTICE	You dance like an old man. Have you ever slept in a bed?
BUTI 1	A what?
JUSTICE	Have you ever eaten with a fork?
BUTI 1	I eat with my hands.
JUSTICE	Do you know what a fork is?
BUTI 1	I don't know.
JUSTICE	Have you heard of a spoon?
BUTI 1	I'm here to learn.
JUSTICE	I don't understand what my father was thinking. Giving me a counsellor who doesn't know a bloody thing.
BUTI 1	I know things.
JUSTICE	Like what.
BUTI 1	Like how to stick fight.
JUSTICE	So?
BUTI 1	I was champion of my village.
JUSTICE	You are no longer in your village.
BUTI 1	I can fight as good as anybody here, I bet.
JUSTICE	I'm the best in this village. Come on. Fight me. What's the matter, old man? Scared?
NELSON	Aside from inheriting this whole new life for myself from my father, I think I inherited something else from him as well. His stubbornness.

The boys assume their stance.

NELSON	Justice was the smartest, most sophisticated and self-assured young man I had ever met. He was everything I was not and desperately wanted to be.
	The fighting begins over the song.
MEN	Khawuze nazo mabhongo Iyoyo mabhong' entliziyo Khawuze nazo kwedini Iyoyo kwedini kabawo Khawuze nazo kwedini Iyoyo kwedini kabawo
WOMEN	Qula kwedini. Qula kwendine quila kwedini kabawo Qula kwedini. Qula kwendine quila kwedini kabawo
	Repeat until JUSTICE knocks BUTI 1 to the ground.
	JUSTICE extends his hand.
JUSTICE	Would you like me to show you that move?
BUTI 1	You would?
JUSTICE	Who better to teach than my own brother?
NELSON	I came to love Justice very much.
	They are brought drinks. BUTI 1 is taken aback.
JUSTICE	To Prince Nelson.
BUTI 1	To Prince Justice.
NELSON	We became the best of friends.
BUTI 1	What is this fence here for?
JUSTICE	It tells you that the land stops here.
BUTI 1	But I see more of it on the other side.
JUSTICE	But it's not ours. This is the end of the Kingdom.
BUTI 1	All of this is yours?
JUSTICE	Ours. Brothers.
BUTI 1	I feel like the luckiest boy in the world.
	Lights shift. JUSTICE presents BUTI 1 with a stick.
JUSTICE	I carved it myself. Welcome to Mqhkezweni. Welcome to your new home.
BUTI 1	Thank you.

JUSTICE	Come on. Let's walk home. Have your heard of a toothbrush?
BUTI 1	No.
JUSTICE	Hmmm.
NELSON	This was an amazing inheritance. I promised myself that I would do my best to make my father proud of me. I saw a whole new universe opening up before me.
BUTI 1	I am in the house of the King. I am a prince. It feels like a dream.
NELSON	My nation believes in sacrifice. So even if you get something for free there is still a sacrifice of equal value that you must give up in return. The greater the gift the greater the sacrifice.

NOSEKENI appears.

BUTI 1	So you will go back and get your things?
NOSEKENI	No, Buti, I am going home.
BUTI 1	This is home.
NOSEKENI	For you. Not for me.
NELSON	Father. Mother.
NOSEKENI	You go back. I can find my way home from here.
BUTI 1	Did Father say when I would be seeing you again?
NOSEKENI	No.
BUTI 1	So this is goodbye?
NOSEKENI	I'm sure it won't be long. Be a good boy.
NELSON	My mother was my first friend. She guided me over my first mountains.
JUSTICE	Come on, Old Man. Let me show you that move.

BUTI 1 starts to run away. NELSON stands in his path and blocks him.

NELSON	Look back. You do not know when you will see her again. Did Father's death teach you nothing about the shortness of life? Look back.
BUTI 1	I'm scared. I want to go home.
NELSON	Look back. You are doing this for her.
	BUTI 1 raises his arms and waves and waves.
BUTI 1	Goodbye, Mother. Goodbye.
NELSON	I said goodbye to a lot that day. My mother. My village. My freedom. All I knew was that I had to do my best and work very hard to make the sacrifice worth it.
JUSTICE	Now let me show you that move.
	The boys raise their sticks.
NELSON	I went to school.
	They fight. BUTI 1 is knocked down.
JUNIOR	You have to push harder. Be aggressive. Stop fighting like an old man.
BUTI 1	Again.
NELSON	I learned all about life at the court of the King.
JUNIOR	I heard that the Minister's daughter asked about you the other day.
BUTI 1	Really?
NELSON	I grew up under the protection of the King.
	BUTI 1 is knocked down.
JUSTICE	No. Never let your guard down, Brother.
BUTI 1	Again.
	The boys fight. BUTI 1 is knocked down again.
NELSON	Nothing ever came easy, but I worked hard to be the type of boy my father loved and respected.
BUTI 1	Again.

> *BUTI 1 is picked up by JUSTICE. They start to fight again.*

JUSTICE   How were your grades this time?

BUTI 1   No C's this time.

JUSTICE   Good. Your game is getting much better.

NELSON   I took to the house of the King like fish to water. It was my home and I thought I was free.

JUSTICE   Look at this my brother.

BUTI 1   What is it?

JUSTICE   Your pass.

BUTI 1   Pass?

JUSTICE   It just lets people know who you are. Look at what it says about you.

BUTI 1   It says my name.

JUSTICE   Look at where it says Father's name.

BUTI 1   King Jongintaba. What is this pass?

JUSTICE   When you travel with Father, as you will, White men will ask to see your pass and you must show it to them. What I have noticed is that when a White man reads who my father is they are nicer to me. Take it. It's yours. Lift your stick and remember what I have taught you. Don't lose it.

NELSON   I wanted to show everybody my pass.

BUTI 1   Father, King Jongintaba…

JUSTICE   Come on. Fight.

> *The boys take their stance.*

BUTI 1   I saw that pretty young girl you were looking at during the last dance.

JUSTICE   Did she ask about me?

> *BUTI 1 knocks JUSTICE down.*

BUTI 1   No. But if I see her again I will tell her you asked.

JUSTICE	*Chong Chong.*
	BUTI 1 extends his hand to JUSTICE who takes it. Lights up on KING and two ELDERs.
KING	Stop playing, my sons.
	The men gather together during the following speech.
NELSON	This new life let me see up close how to rule. When there were important issues affecting our nation, Father would send out letters to all the head men informing them of the meetings. They would inform all of the other men and in a few days the whole Kingdom would arrive. Father would greet all of the guests and then each of them would have a chance to speak. Father would not speak again until the end of the session. This idea of democracy affected me greatly in years to come. I had a wonderful education and a wonderful future before me.
KING	Childhood is over. It is time for you both to become men.
NELSON	Time had flown.
BUTI 1	What if I flinch?
JUSTICE	You won't.
BUTI 1	But I might.
NELSON	To become men we had to pass a test. This test symbolised the final stage of childhood for each boy in the village, and the final stage of childhood and the first test of our manhood. A boy who did not pass this test would never be a fully integrated member of the tribe. He would never be able to marry. He could never have children. Most importantly he would never have the respect of his fellow men.
BUTI 1	I am scared that I might…
JUSTICE	Don't worry about it.
BUTI 1	You always say that.
JUSTICE	And you worry like an old woman.

BUTI 1   I have heard it hurts.

NELSON   Each of us had to build a hut. In the hut we were told to place all of our childhood memories. Once the hut was built we sat in the hut reflecting on our childhood years.

BUTI 1   Look back.

NELSON   On the day of the ceremony we were led to the river to wash. To purify our bodies like we had purified our minds.

BUTI 1   I'm still scared.

JUSTICE   Don't be. I hear it is over before you know it.

NELSON   Then we were called forward.

> *The CHORUS enters, dressed in the ceremonial attire, and take their place. NELSON assumes the role of an ELDER.*

This spear has been sharpened razor thin. With the tip of this spear I will cut off your foreskin. The elders will follow close behind to stare into your eyes. They must not see any fear.

> *The ELDER passes in front of each man and mimes the cutting. Once the cutting is complete each man cries out "I am a man." The first CHORUS member should do this in English and the second in Xhosa on down the line until NELSON reaches BUTI 1 & BUTI 2. The following lines are done as a voiceover:*

BUTI 1   I must not flinch.

NELSON   They must not see your eyes water.

BUTI 1   Do not flinch.

NELSON   They must not see a muscle move.

BUTI 1   Be a man.

BUTI 2   Must not flinch.

BUTI 1   I want to scream.

BUTI 2   Must not flinch.

BUTI 1	This pain is unbearable.
BUTI 2	Don't flinch. Be a man.
BUTI 1	I want to go home.
NELSON	*Rolihlahla.*
BOTH	Yes?
NELSON	Hurry up, boy. Say it.
BUTI 2	*Ndi do ta. (Translation: I am a man.)*

Lights fade on BUTI 1.

I'm a man.

NELSON	I was sixteen years old. Justice was twenty one. I was a man now. The world transformed and dreams formed that I could claim.
BUTI 2	I want a job with the government, a pretty wife, and a house full of children. Money to help my mother and serve my tribe. A job with the government, a pretty wife, and a house full of children. To be a great councillor to the King.
NELSON	You are now men. Childhood is over. Set your huts on fire.

BUTI 1 walks to his hut. He stands there crying. BUTI 2 sets the hut on fire.

Song:

MEN	Ndinomhle. Ndinomt'omhle. Ndinomt'omhle. Ndinomt'omhle. Ntombazanamolo. Ntombazanamolo. Ntombazanamolo. Ntombazanamolo uzawlibon'izulu uyawamemeza Uyawmemeza. Ntombazanamolo. Ntombazanamolo. Ntombazanamolo. Ntombazanamolo uzawlibon'szulu uyawamemeza Uyawamemeza.
WOMEN	Ndinosana Iwam' usana Iwam'Ndinebhongo ngosana Iwam'

> Ndinosana Iwam' usana Iwam'Ndinebhongo ngosana
> Iwam'

NELSON   Such dreams. Such sacrifice.

KING   The Elder has come to say a few words to our men.

NELSON   I had just come to the base of another mountain.

ELDER   There they sit. The sons of the tribe. We have accorded them the status of men. There they sit with the great gift of manhood and nowhere to use it.

BUTI 2   What was this Elder saying?

ELDER   There are farmers who will never have any land to raise a crop. There are scholars who will never teach because there is no place for them to study.

NELSON   This was sacrilege.

ELDER   There are Kings who will never rule because they themselves are subject to the rules of the British. Let us not fool ourselves into thinking that this ritual means anything to these men. Most of them will go off to the city where they work for the White man for pennies. They will waste away in the deep holes of the diamond mines where their lungs will be filled with poison and they will die. If that does not kill them then they will waste away living in shacks and drinking cheap alcohol. Because we are a defeated people. We are renters on our own land. We are slaves in our own country.

BUTI 2   That is not true.

NELSON   Or was it?

ELDER   Here we sit this evening under the moonlight given us by the Great God Qamata. He who never sleeps and watches over us day and night. But I think this God of ours is asleep. For if he is watching us he cannot like what he is seeing. We have just put these young men through the rites of manhood and in doing so have promised them a future, but I do not see a future for any of these men.

Reaction from the crowd.

Qamata must be asleep. I wish that I could die so I could go to Qamata and shake him awake and tell him, the flower of the Xhosa nation is dying. The men have no future. These men have no land. These men have no possibilities. We have lied to them. I want to see our Great God Qamata so I can shake him awake and tell him to do something. The flower of the nation is dying. *Embali y sez e a fa.*

KING *E yanni ma sa ben ne.*

Silence. BUTI 2 rises and runs off. JUSTICE follows. Lights shift.

JUSTICE You can't run back, Buti. There is nothing but ashes.

BUTI 2 He is a mean, stupid old man. He knows nothing. What does he know? He can't even read.

JUSTICE Then you have no reason to be upset.

BUTI 2 You heard what he said.

JUSTICE It was painful.

BUTI 2 They were lies.

JUSTICE Were they?

BUTI 2 Teachers who will not teach. Scholars who will never learn. I am in school. I am going to get my degree.

JUSTICE You are lucky. I am lucky.

BUTI 2 All of this is yours.

JUSTICE Look over there, Buti. Look on the other side of that fence. Do you see all of that land?

BUTI 2 Yes.

JUSTICE It used to belong to us.

BUTI 2 He ruined everything.

JUSTICE One day, Buti, you will see that I am a man with just a few acres.

NELSON	A seed was planted in me. A seed that I was not prepared to water.
JUSTICE	When you are a real man, you will understand what he is saying.
BUTI 2	What is on the other side of that river?
JUSTICE	The rest of the world that we will never see. Johannesburg.
NELSON	My tribe had made me what I was, and I was a man of the tribe, and I was determined to prove that old fool wrong. But fate stepped in and changed the course I was to take. I was kicked out of school. I had run afoul of the administration over a protest and was sent home. If I agreed to cooperate I would be let back in school, if I did not, then I could never return.
BUTI 2	There are other schools for me to attend.
KING	Name one.
BUTI 2	There are schools all over this country.
KING	For Whites. Not for you.
BUTI 2	You are a King….
KING	I am an African King. Welcome to South Africa. I thought you understood at least that much. I can only do so much and I am begging you to go back and finish. Get your degree. Such are the limits of an African King.
BUTI 2	It's not fair.
KING	Stop thinking of yourself and think of your poor mother. Be a man.
BUTI 2	I will see that she is looked after.
KING	How?
BUTI 2	I don't know.
KING	Well I do.
JUSTICE	Father, maybe if we just give…

KING	You be quiet. You who have graduated from school and spends all of his time in idle pursuits is not one to talk to me about responsibility. I am disgusted with the both of you. It is time you started behaving like men, and as your father, not your King, I am going to make sure that you do just that. You are both to be married.
JUSTICE	Marry?
BUTI 2	Who?
KING	As your father I have the right to determine who and when you will marry.
NELSON	We knew both of these girls. The one who I was supposed to marry was in love with Justice. The other one was… ugly.
BUTI 2	This is grossly unfair.
KING	It is my right.
BUTI 2	We should have some say in this matter.
KING	You are the ones who are throwing your lives away. It is my job as your father to see that you start to behave like men. It is my right.
JUSTICE	We should have some say…
KING	I will not be moved on this subject. There will be no more discussion.
	The KING exits.
NELSON	I saw a miserable future for myself. Me with a wife that did not love me, forced to live together in a house we both did not want. It would be a prison. It was not fair.
BUTI 2	No.
JUSTICE	There is no way out of this one.
BUTI 2	Don't be such a defeatist. There is a way.
JUSTICE	I'd like to know what it is.
BUTI 2	Leave.

JUSTICE	And go where, my brother?
BUTI 2	Johannesburg.
JUSTICE	You would do that, Nelson?
BUTI 2	I'm not going to ruin my life. My wife-to-be loves you.
JUSTICE	And mine is ugly as sin but…
BUTI 2	What? Are you going to flinch Justice? Aren't we men now? Can't we decide our own fate?
JUSTICE	We need money.

> *Short pause.*

BUTI 2	Father's prize bull.
JUSTICE	You are kidding.
BUTI 2	If we want to leave we have to be serious. We can sell the bull to the neighbouring farmer. He is always asking Father to sell it. We will steal it and that will give us enough money to get to Johannesburg.
JUSTICE	Father will kill us.
BUTI 2	He has to find us first.
JUSTICE	I did not know you had this in you, Madiba.
BUTI 2	Wasn't Father seeing about getting you a job in the mines?
JUSTICE	Yes. He had a position arranged for me in the office.
BUTI 2	Do you think they would take me on as well?
JUSTICE	We could see.
BUTI 2	Once they read our passes how can they say no?
JUSTICE	Nelson…
BUTI 2	You want to get married?
NELSON	We stole the bull. We sold the bull. We got on the train to Johannesburg.

> *Lights shift.*

JUSTICE	We are free as the wind, Brother. Do you have your pass?
BUTI 2	Yes.
NELSON	I thought I was a free man.
	NOSEKENI begins to sing the South African National Anthem.
BUTI 2	I love this place Justice. I grew up here. It is my home.
JUSTICE	Father will get over his anger.
BUTI 2	I hope so.
NELSON	Childhood was now officially over.
JUSTICE	Look forward my brother. There is nothing back there for you but ashes.
BUTI 2	I see the mountains, and I am going to climb every one of them.
JUSTICE	Don't look back. Johannesburg awaits. The streets are paved with gold. Look forward.
BUTI 2	To Johannesburg.
JUSTICE	We are free.
NELSON	A new dream was about to begin.

Act 2

NELSON   Dreams guide you, delude you, surprise you. We
              were our dreams made flesh, and on the ride to
              Johannesburg our dreams were wild with possibilities.
              Johannesburg was a dream, a big gold dream for Justice
              and me.

              Lights up. Music. Up tempo. Dancing.

              A city of gold. A place where, if you worked hard
              enough, an African could make his dream come true.

JUSTICE   We need to get to the mines.

              *The crowd leads JUSTICE and BUTI 2 on a tour.
              The set becomes alive with the urban landscape.*

NELSON   There was a pulse to this city. Cars alongside the
              horse-drawn wagons. Africans were striving for
              something. Zulus, Xhosa, Sotho, British, Boer, Pondo,
              together making something new.

              *A dance of city life transpires. It reaches a point of
              great abandon. Suddenly the music stops. A White
              policeman enters.*

POLICEMAN   Passes. Have your passes ready.

              *Everybody African reaches into their pockets, purses,
              baskets etc. to get their passes. The POLICEMAN
              scans them all. He reaches BUTI 2, and the Young
              WOMAN BUTI 2 was speaking with last. BUTI 2
              shows his pass. The policeman says nothing. He
              approaches the Young WOMAN. The policeman stops.*

              Come here. I know you all are all supposed to look
              alike but even I can see this is not you. This is not
              your pass.

Y. WOMAN   Then I must have picked up the wrong one by mistake
              at home. I'll go home and get it.

POLICEMAN   Shut up.

Y. WOMAN   If you let me go home… my mother is there and
I can…

POLICEMAN   Did I tell you to shut your Black mouth?

Y. WOMAN   Please, sir, I need to get to work today…

*POLICEMAN slaps the woman to the ground. The
crowd grows tense.*

POLICEMAN   Get up. Get up.

BUTI 2 moves to help her.

Do you want some of this as well?

BUTI 2   No Baas…

POLICEMAN   Carry on then. Get up. Get up. I said disperse. This is
none of your concern. Disperse. NOW.

NELSON   A pass. Back home the police would be nicer to me,
because they read who my father was. In Johannesburg
it mattered very little. I was a *kaffir* like the rest of the
brethren. This was my first introduction to the world
that lay outside my village. The real and brutal world
of African men and women. This pass was no more
than a leash around our necks. It told us where we
could go, how long we could stay, where we could
work, where we could live. It was not a leash. It was
a noose around the neck of every African person in
the country.

*Each person holds out their pass for inspection. The
POLICEMAN walks down the line. All is in order.
The POLICEMAN exits. The crowd makes sure he is
gone. The music resumes and the dancing resumes.*

JUSTICE   Pay no attention.

BUTI 2   How much farther to the mines?

*A large sign descends. It reads "Crown Mines." The
lights shift. The sound shifts. The crowd disperses.*

NELSON   If any place can rob you of your dreams, it's a gold
mine. I pictured a place of calm where large boulders

of gold sat waiting for me to ship all over the world. A place of joy. A place of laughter.

Muffled explosions. A man is dragged onstage and dumped.

What I saw was a war zone. Great deep pits. The sounds of explosions. Metal grinding against metal and grinding against rock. The land ripped to pieces. A mine looks like hell on earth. To work in the office was considered very good. To enter the pits meant certain death.

MINERs chant.

MINER		CHORUS	
	Abelungu		Ngodem ngodem
	Basibiza		Ngojim ngojim
	Hooo		Ngodem ngodem
	Basibiza		Ngojim ngojim
	Hooo		Ziyasha ziyasha
	Qubula		Ziyasha ziyasha

Repeated until MINERs exit.

The FOREMAN enters.

FOREMAN	What do you want?
JUSTICE	I am Justice. Son of King…
FOREMAN	Yes?
JUSTICE	I have come to take my position…
FOREMAN	You were not due to arrive for three months.
JUSTICE	My father sent me early…
FOREMAN	Your father did not mention it to me…
JUSTICE	He is sending you a letter
FOREMAN	So your father is sending a letter to me. Is that right Nelson?
JUSTICE	I said it was true. My word…

FOREMAN	Read this. It is a communication that I received from your father.

JUSTICE takes the message. He reads it. JUSTICE hands it to BUTI 2. BUTI 2 reads it.

BUTI 2	Send boys home immediately.
JUSTICE	I am sure that we can…
FOREMAN	Get out and I never want to see your faces in this mine ever again. Leave.

Shift. A city street. The pace is more realistic. Horse hoofs clopping. Car horns beeping. The sound of the mine in the distance.

	What is that man doing lying there?
MAN 1	He's dead sir.
FOREMAN	Are you sure?
MAN 1	Yes sir.
FOREMAN	Put the body out of the bloody way. Find out his name so I can notify the family.
MAN 1	Yes Mamma kus.
BUTI 2	Justice, that man…
JUSTICE	Just be glad it isn't you.
NELSON	The reality of Johannesburg snuffed out any of the dreams that I held on the train. It was not going to be easy. To be the son of a King meant very little. Whatever I achieved I would have to achieve on my own and through my own hard work.

FOREMAN becomes POLICEMAN.

POLICEMAN	*(offstage)* Passes please.
BUTI 2	We have no money and no place to stay.
JUSTICE	There is a Minister…
BUTI 2	If we had told the truth we would have jobs.

JUSTICE	So we will go to the Minister. He is a friend of Father's and…
BUTI 2	Lie to a Minister…
JUSTICE	You want to go back? We need a place to stay.
BUTI 2	I have a cousin here.
JUSTICE	We came here together.
NELSON	Some dreams fall apart. Justice and I set about our different paths. My cousin took me to Walter Sisulu. He sent clients to a man named Walter Sidelsky.

Phone rings. Lights up on SECRETARY on the phone.

SECRETARY	Witkin, Sidelsky and Eidelman. Attorneys at Law. How can I help you.

BUTI 2 gives the SECRETARY his pass as a sign is lowered in. It reads "Witkin, Sidelsky and Eidelman. Attorneys at Law."

NELSON	I was given a job as a clerk in the office and I enrolled in school so I could get my degree. This office was to be a wonderful training ground for me.
SECRETARY	That should be enough for the officials. It outlines where you work, and the hours of work. The only thing missing is Mr. Sidelsky's signature. You can have a seat, Nelson. I bought you a little present. I got you your own cup.

SECRETARY pulls out a black cup.

BUTI 2	Thank you.
SECRETARY	I keep all of the tea cups on a tray in the kitchen.
NELSON	There was a tray of white cups and black cups next to the stove.
SECRETARY	I'm just going to put this cup along with all of the others.
NELSON	I had a black cup.
SECRETARY	I have to ask one favour, Nelson. Please make sure that you only drink out of this cup. If you break it I

have others the same colour in my desk…. Some of
our clients can be really funny about these things.
They ask. Okay? It's not right but it's what it is. We
all can drink our tea out here together though.

> *WALTER and SIDELSKY enter.*

SECRETARY   The pass is ready for you to sign.

SIDELSKY   *(to WALTER)* You'll take care of these depositions.

> *SIDELSKY moves to the desk and signs it. WALTER
> enters and bows to BUTI 2. Somehow there is a pause
> in here. The signing of the pass. The bowing of the
> man. The two Whites look on with interest.*

WALTER   Did you know that his father is a King?

SIDELSKY   No.

WALTER   And here he is carrying a pass and being hired as
a gopher in your office.

SIDELSKY   I run a fair and democratic office. *(hands NELSON his
pass)*

WALTER   You people stole our land from us and then make us
pay through the nose to get the worst parts of it back.
How fair is that Sidelsky?

SIDELSKY   Time will take care of that.

WALTER   Time can mean another man's whole life, Sidelsky.

SIDELSKY   If we don't create a neutral ground there can be no
gathering place. Welcome aboard Nelson. Anything
you need, you let me know. The pass is all signed. No
hard feelings?

WALTER   No.

SIDELSKY   Neutral ground.

SECRETARY   I'll put the kettle on.

NELSON   Walter was a new kind of man to me. He had his own
business. He did not bow down to Whites and he
knew things. Not out of books but from life. He had
lived. He spoke his mind. *(The phone rings.)*

SIDELSKY	I'll take it in my office. Stay for tea.
	BUTI 2 gets up and is angry.
WALTER	What's the matter with you.
BUTI 2	They have two sets of cups.
WALTER	So. They have two sets of cups.
BUTI 2	One for the Whites and one for us. I was told that I could only drink out of a black cup.
	SECRETARY runs in. She opens her drawer and pulls out a black cup.
SECRETARY	Stay for tea?
	WALTER smiles. SECRETARY exits.
WALTER	She told you that you could not drink out of the white cups?
BUTI 2	Yes.
WALTER	Then just do as I do.
	SECRETARY enters with trays of cups and a pot of tea. SIDELSKY enters.
WALTER	I do love a cup of tea this time of day.
SECRETARY	Help yourself, Mr. Sisulu.
	WALTER picks up a white cup and make a deliberate cup of tea. The response is shocked. SIDELSKY looks on.
WALTER	Nelson, won't you have a cup?
BUTI 2	I'm not thirsty.
NELSON	I was going to change the laws. If the laws were unfair then that was the logical place for me to start. It could all be achieved through rational argument and reason. From the inside so to speak. Work with other educated men to make the society one of justice and freedom. You could achieve nothing if you made the others mad at you.

WALTER	I'll see everybody tomorrow. If you need anything, Nelson you let me know okay? No hard feelings? Thank you for the tea.
SIDELSKY	Neutral ground.
WALTER	Thank you for the wonderful cup of tea.
	WALTER exits.
SIDELSKY	Take a bit of advice from me, Nelson. Do not get involved in politics. It can do horrible things to men. Run along with the documents. If you go to the entrance at the back of the building you'll find your way in.
	BUTI 2 exits.
NELSON	I completed my degree and got accepted to study law. One of the few Africans allowed to do so.
	WALTER enters.
BUTI 2	This is fantastic news.
WALTER	All your dreams are coming true. Good for you. I'm going to have to cancel boxing tonight. I have a meeting I have to go to.
NELSON	I was hoping that we could celebrate.
WALTER	You can come if you like. We can go out after the meeting. It's an ANC meeting.
NELSON	I had heard of this organisation of course. From what I had heard, these people were a group of troublemakers.
BUTI 2	Some other time, Walter.
NELSON	Most of them ended up in prison on Robben Island. No way. Not me. I had dreams. A house. Some land. A wife. Children. Making my father proud of me. But first, my law degree.
	Lights up on Law PROFESSOR. BUTI 2 hands his pass to "The Law PROFESSOR."

PROFESSOR	Law is a very complicated and technical field of endeavour. It requires a nimble mind and keen intelligence. In short, I think there is no place for women or for Blacks in the study of law.
BUTI 2	I believe the Nazis said the same thing about Jews?
PROFESSOR	I'm not a racist. You just can't accept the truth.
BUTI 2	That I am not as good as you are?
PROFESSOR	Your grades, Mr. Mandela, only back up my theory.

Law PROFESSOR returns BUTI 2's pass to him.

Welcome to my class.

NELSON   He was right. I was a horrible student, but I worked hard. It is not pleasant being the only Black in a room full of Whites. I would go into class each day and sit alone because none of these future lawyers would sit next to me. But on campus I met many people of other races who were different. People who believed in a better world for everybody, and who were willing to do something to fight the injustice that they saw around them.

The chant begins as the lights go up on JUSTICE. Chant is recorded.

CHORUS   Siyolo
Xoxo
Stowkwe
Tembu
Ndlambe
Ngqika
Hintsa
Gadla Henry
Gadla Henry

JUSTICE   I have to go home.

BUTI 2   That would be nice. If I can get the money maybe during the next break we can go back home and relax and have some…. What is it?

JUSTICE   Father…

BUTI 2	He can't send you back home now. You are here. Right? We have made a life for ourselves now. We are men.
JUSTICE	He's dead. I have to go home.
BUTI 2	We both have to go home.
NELSON	The loss of my father the King affected me greatly. Here was a man who took me under his wing and sheltered me. Even after the disgraceful way that I behaved he...
	The sound of the train.
BUTI 2	I am graduating from Law School soon. I'd be honoured if my King came to the ceremony?
JUSTICE	Your King?
BUTI 2	The King is dead. Long live the King.
	JUSTICE and BUTI 2 hug. Lights shift. BUTI 2 looks out the back of the train. JUSTICE waves. The lights on the men's CHORUS fades.
NELSON	I graduated from Law School.
BUTI 2	Your Honour. The gentleman in question merely forgot his pass.
NELSON	I set up my law practice.
BUTI 2	He did not hurt anybody. He did not kill anyone.
NELSON	I had more than enough clients, and for the first time I was able to send my mother money every week.
BUTI 2	How many times have you forgotten your keys, Your Honour?
JUDGE	Forgetting keys is not against the law. Forgetting your pass is.
BUTI 2	And just where did you leave your pass this morning your honour?
JUDGE	Law is about reality. The reality is that this man did not have his pass with him. The law states that he is

	to have it with him at all times. He did not have his pass and that is a criminal offense.
BUTI 2	But if you send this man to prison his children will not be able to eat.
JUDGE	He should have thought about that before he forgot his pass. I sentence your client to one year in jail. Do you have your pass Mr. Mandela?

BUTI 2 shows his pass. WALTER enters.

WALTER	You want to represent your people?
BUTI 2	I do represent them.
WALTER	How?
BUTI 2	I'm a lawyer. I offer them services, and they look up to me.
WALTER	And for that support and prestige you get what?
BUTI 2	I get paid.
WALTER	And what do they get back from you?
BUTI 2	You have a point to make, then make it.
WALTER	You lost a case today?
BUTI 2	He got a year in jail. One whole year for nothing. The fellow before him got two years.
WALTER	Is that your idea of progress? Is that all? One less year of suffering?
BUTI 2	What's your idea?
WALTER	My dream is an end of suffering.
BUTI 2	Come and tell me.
WALTER	About what?
BUTI 2	The troublemakers.
WALTER	Amandla.
CHORUS	Ngawethu.
WALTER	Amandla.

CHORUS   Ngawethu.

WALTER   The African National Congress is an organisation of
peaceful protest. We do not believe that Blacks should
rule Whites or that Blacks should rule the Coloureds
and the Coloureds should rule the rest of us. We
believe in fairness and justice for everybody. The
organisation is open to everybody and anybody who
shares our dream. You have a story to tell us, Sister.
Please do.

VOICE   Tell us, Sister.

Lights up on WOMAN.

WOMAN   Every day I get up at four o'clock in the morning.
I comb my daughter's hair while she is still asleep,
so it will look nice for school that day. I make
breakfast for the children and by quarter to five
I am waiting at the bus stop to go to work. By the
time the bus arrives at my stop it is already full.
I stand in the aisle for an hour and a half. That is how
long it takes for me to get to the back door of my
madam's house. I get her children out of bed. I make
them breakfast. I clean the house. I make the madam
breakfast. I do the laundry. I clean some more. I iron
the clothes. I make lunches. I cook dinner. If I am
lucky I can get home in time to see my children off to
bed. Most nights I am not that lucky. I spend one full
day with my children each week. Only Sunday.

The fares for the buses are high. If these fares rise then
I will not be able to take the bus to work. I will have
to live in the madam's house or be fired. Jobs are hard
to find. If I have to live in, who will look after my
children for me? Who is going to comb my little girl's
hair for school?

SPEAKER   That story can be told one hundred times over. There
is an election coming up, and we have to let these
people know the fact that we don't vote does not
mean we have no voice in the affairs of this country.
That story is our mothers' story. That story is our
sisters' story.

BUTI 2	And that story cannot be my daughters' story or my sons'.
WALTER	We must stand up and fight this measure.
VOICE 1	Let our voice be heard.
VOICE 2	But how? How do we do this?
VOICE 3	Boycott. Boycott.
WALTER	Do not take the bus to work. Do not go to work. Shut the city down. Make them see that we cannot vote but we still have a voice. Let that voice be heard.
NELSON	The Bus Boycott was my first foray into public protest.

Signs that read "Bus fare hike unfair." Lights up on WM, an announcer.

WM	I can't believe it. The city is at a virtual standstill as the bus boycott continues. Offices are closed. Buses are empty. Housewives have lost their maids. Hotels are complaining that there is nobody to clean the rooms and change the sheets for the guests. The bus company is losing millions of rands in revenue and the belligerent strikers will not budge.

Lights fade on WM. The company sings a protest song/chant. The march should come alive. Lights shift. WM enters as POLICEMAN. The song/chant ends.

POLICEMAN	Get on the bus.
WALTER	We do not believe in violence.

Song.

POLICEMAN	Get on the bus.
WALTER	The ANC does not believe in violence.
POLICEMAN	Get on the bus. Get on it. Now.
WALTER	Freedom for all of us. Harmony. Harmony.

There is a great defiance in the previous moment within the tone and volume of the song. The POLICEMAN backs down and walks away. Silence. Celebration.

> *Lights up on WALTER and NELSON.*

Well.

BUTI 2 We won.

WALTER We won?

BUTI 2 We won. We did it. I didn't believe it. No bloodshed. Just voices.

WALTER So you are going to add your voice to the song?

BUTI 2 I like to win.

WALTER So do we.

BUTI 2 Amandla.

CHORUS Ngawethu.

BUTI 2 Amandla.

CHORUS Ngawethu.

> *A song of celebration.*

NELSON It really was a new day. We had won the fight. I was in love. After the victory I was happy to join. I was in love with this movement and I could see results.

WALTER Nelson I have somebody I would like you to meet. Evelyn Mase.

> *Lights up on EVELYN. A romantic song of the period underscores the following scene.*

NELSON Educated. A nurse. She was a very nice person. Everything I ever dreamed of in a woman. I fell in love.

EVELYN I would like a house.

BUTI 2 Me too.

EVELYN Children.

BUTI 2 Of course.

EVELYN A real family.

NELSON Evelyn had lost both her parents as a child.

EVELYN	A normal life.
BUTI 2	In a few years I see us expanding the practice. I see us being able to have a house. I see myself coming home for dinner each night. I see children running under my feet. I tickle them, they tickle me back. I see us retiring together when we are older in Qunu.
EVELYN	I see a garden. Fresh meat. Walls freshly painted each year. Room for all of us. Home. That's all I want. A sweet and loving home.

They kiss. NOSEKENI enters and begins to sing a lullaby.

NELSON	We married and in time I had a son. The world was a brighter place. Again, the dreams were made of flesh. In the eyes of a child shines the pure light of possibilities.
BUTI 2	He has his grandfather's eyes.
NELSON	In the deep brown eyes and kinky hair of my son I saw the possibilities for the future I had started fighting for.
BUTI 2	I will call him Madiba. My clan name.
NELSON	A light.
BUTI 2	Madiba Thembekile. Thembi.
NELSON	Now I was a real man. All my dreams had come true.

WALTER enters with a sign. It reads "Niggers in their place."

There had been an election. A new government had come to power.

BUTI 2	What is this?
WALTER	This, my friend, is Apartheid. This Government has lost its mind.
NELSON	Mother used to say you cannot run from the setting of the sun. You cannot run from the darkness.
BUTI 2	What are we going to do?

WALTER	Fight.
BUTI 2	Evelyn take Thembi. I have to go.
EVELYN	Where are you…
BUTI 2	I have to go. Take the baby.

The following chant underscores the POLICEMAN's speech that follows.

WALTER	Amandla.
CHORUS	Ngawethu.
WALTER	Amandla.
CHORUS	Ngawethu.
BUTI 2	Amandla.

POLICEMAN enters with bullhorn making the following announcement. He plants a sign that reads "Whites Only."

POLICEMAN The Group Areas Act. Under this new law certain locations are designated Whites only and others for Blacks and so on. Blacks are forbidden to own homes or land in any White area and so forth and so on.

Can't you read?

BUTI 2 Whites only.

POLICEMAN Move along.

BUTI 2 But my law office is in that building.

POLICEMAN Was in that building. Under the new law this is a White building. No Blacks are allowed to rent or own… move along…

BUTI 2 I have paid my rent six months in advance.

POLICEMAN Can't you read?

BUTI 2 This is against the law.

POLICEMAN You can read the sign. If you have a problem, go and make an appeal to the magistrate.

POLICEMAN exits.

BUTI 2   Minister, I was asked to come before you to request that you review my case. I am a lawyer. I'm thirty-five years old. I have a young son and we have just had a daughter. I have built up a thriving practice in the heart of the city. You must know how desperate my community is for legal services. My office is crowded each and every day. People need me to be in a place where they can find me. Sir, if I'm to be moved....

Lights up on WM.

WM   Request denied. The law is the law.

Blackout. EVELYN enters holding a baby.

EVELYN   Hold Makaziwe.

BUTI 2   They want to move me to some place miles outside of town. My clients can't reach me there.

EVELYN   So what does this mean? Take the baby.

BUTI 2   It means that I have to start over again.

EVELYN   The Lord will provide.

BUTI 2   He provided, but the government has taken it all away.

EVELYN   Maybe you could find another line of work.

BUTI 2   This was my dream. To be a lawyer. I had a practice and... I can't just sit by and let this happen to me. It's our dream.

EVELYN   The laws are the laws.

BUTI 2   If they are unfair then they have to be changed.

EVELYN   And where will that lead you? I know where. To prison. And then what? You run out of here every evening to go to meetings and what have you accomplished? Nothing. You need to look at the world as it is. The laws are in place and they will stay in place and we have to find a way to work within them. Put your faith in God, Nelson. Take your troubles to him and he will work it out for you. We can find a way.

BUTI 2	Not by kneeling.
EVELYN	We had a dream, Nelson. We wanted the same thing…
BUTI 2	And this government is going to ensure that we never get it.
EVELYN	We will get it in the next life.
BUTI 2	Wake up.
EVELYN	You wake up. Do you know what your son wanted to know the other day? Do you know what he asked me?
BUTI 2	What?
EVELYN	Where you lived. That is reality, Nelson Mandela. That is our life and our home.
BUTI 2	I have to do this.
EVELYN	That is why they would not renew your last appeal. You make them mad with all of this…
NELSON	The movement had become my life.
EVELYN	You can stay home this one evening. You promised to take Thembi to box with you. Hold your daughter.
	THEMBI enters.
THEMBI	Father, are you ready to go boxing?
BUTI 2	Tomorrow.
THEMBI	We'll go tomorrow.
NELSON	Tomorrow.
THEMBI	You said that last time. I thought you said a man is no better than his word.
WM	In accordance with the group areas act, the section of Johannesburg known as Sophiatown is being torn down. Blacks are no longer allowed to live in the city unless authorised.
BUTI 2	They are kicking us out of our homes. Tomorrow, Thembi. We will box tomorrow. I promise.

EVELYN	Nelson… Nelson… Nelson please…
BUTI 2	Amandla.
CHORUS	Ngawethu.

Lights shift. The sound of flame. Lights up on three barrels filled with light. Fire. The people sing. They take their passes and throw them in the fire. BUTI 2 drops his pass into the fire. Song continues during NELSON's speech.

CHORUS	*Senzenina. Senzenina. Senzenina na senzenina.*
NELSON	Sophiatown was the African section of Johannesburg. This neighbourhood had been here for generations. It was my home. People had built homes. Now. Suddenly. They were ripped off of their land and told to live someplace else. No compensation. No recompense.
BUTI 2	We are going to light a fire.

Lights shift. Three barrels are revealed. They have red light coming from inside of them.

We are going to form a line and burn our passes.

The CHORUS does this.

The ANC does not believe in violence.

NELSON	I had a son. I had to teach him what it was to be a man.

NELSON throws his pass into the fire. Silence. Machine gun fire. Tanks. Helicopters. War. Screams. BUTI 2 enters his home area.

EVELYN	Where were you…
BUTI 2	The less you know, the better.
EVELYN	Where are you going?
BUTI 2	This is something that must be done.
EVELYN	No matter what it does to our family?
BUTI 2	I'm trying to make a better world.

EVELYN	Better world? A better world for who? I'm unhappy. The children don't even know you and…
BUTI 2	I don't have time for this. I have to go.
EVELYN	Where?
BUTI 2	You are my wife. You are not the police. I will contact you…
EVELYN	Yes I know. Tomorrow. I used to live for that too.

Lights out on EVELYN.

NELSON	We protested more and more. Peace was met with slaughter.
BUTI 2	They are killing us in cold blood, Walter.
WALTER	I was there.
BUTI 2	These non violent tactics are not going to work. You saw what they did. You saw what they are.
WALTER	That's not our way.
BUTI 2	It's not my way either, but we can't just take this.
WALTER	I'm not killing anybody Nelson. It's that simple. The organisation will not go for it. Once we spill a White person's blood it's going to be war.
BUTI 2	We have bled buckets, Walter. They have declared war on us. We must do something to let them know that we have some power. The aim of our violence is not to kill. It is to disrupt. Make them see that they have to deal with us.
WALTER	It's not like they are leaving us much choice.
BUTI 2	My father always said that you could defeat a man and not take away his dignity. They are trying to take our dignity, Walter, and I will not let them. We are men. Amandla.
CHORUS	Ngawethu.

	(*singing*) Sibatshelile wema	Welele ma
	Uyez'u Umkohonto we Sizwe	Welele ma
	Uyez'u Nelson Mandela	Welele ma

	Uyez'u Tata	Welele ma
	Uyez'u Nelson Mandela	Welele ma

Repeat until song shifts to "Toyi Toyi."

NELSON   One thing about me never changed.

BUTI 2   The Spear of the Nation.

NELSON   I could never resist a good fight.

Explosion.

Umkhonto we Sizwe. The military wing of the African National Congress.

CHORUS shifts song to "Toyi Toyi," a call and response piece performed by everybody.

ALL

Oliver Tambo	Uyah e wey	**CHORUS**	Hi Hi
Winnie Mandela	Uyah e wey		Hi Hi
Walter Sisulu	Uyah e wey		Hi Hi
Nelson Mandela	Uyah e wey		Hi Hi
	Hi Hi Hi		
	Hi Hi Hi		

Two explosions.

NELSON   The Spear of the Nation was born.

POLICEMAN   Nelson Mandela and Walter Sisulu along with other members in the leadership of the ANC are public enemy number one. If anybody has seen or heard about the whereabouts of either of these men please inform the police immediately.

NELSON   All I wanted was for each member of my society to have an opportunity to participate as full members. As true citizens of their country. At first I just wanted my dreams, and over time my dreams for myself became the dreams for the country. I loved this country with all of my heart. I loved the land like I loved my family. Now I found myself a criminal. I had lost my ability to make a living. I had lost...

BUTI 2 runs on.

BUTI 2   Evelyn. Evelyn, I know you heard what they are saying about me on the radio and… hello… Thembi… Evelyn…

NELSON   Families were torn apart daily. Children were left without mothers because their mother had been relocated and children were not allowed to be with her. A father was arrested and while he was in jail his wife and children were relocated and he had no idea where to find them.

I was a fugitive now. I went into hiding.

Man 1 enters with a bag of food.

WALTER   Food. Keep your head down.

BUTI 2   How long do you think…

WALTER   We have to get out of the country.

BUTI 2   I don't want to go.

WALTER   You don't have a choice. Take the food. You are no good to anyone dead.

BUTI 2 takes the food. He picks up a bottle of milk. He prepares the bottle during the following speech. He opens the bottle. He gets on his hands and knees very carefully. Taking great precautions not to be seen, he places the bottle of milk in a special light. A windowsill.

NELSON   One of the best loved foods of my people is curdled milk. It's like a cottage cheese. I was being hidden in the home of a White man. (*NELSON puts his carton of milk on the rim of the boxing rim. He goes back to jumping rope.*) You have to wait at least a day to eat it. You just leave the carton on the windowsill for a day and you come back to cheese. I set the carton on the windowsill. A policeman was passing one day and saw this on the window sill. I had forgotten… only Africans ate this dish.

The bottle of milk is tipped.

GUARD   Come out with your hands up. The house is surrounded.

> *BUTI 2 raises his hands over his head. Lights up on*
> *THEMBI.*

THEMBI I can read the paper now, Mother. Father's in jail.

EVELYN Then you know everything.

THEMBI Mother?

EVELYN Yes?

THEMBI What's treason?

NELSON The Rivonia Treason Trial. I was arrested and charged with treason against the state. The maximum one could get if convicted was death.

THEMBI Daddy always says that he loves this country.

EVELYN He does.

THEMBI But they arrested him. He's a criminal.

EVELYN No. He believes in saving this country for you.

THEMBI And you don't?

EVELYN I believe in saving your life until his dreams for you can come true.

THEMBI There is no tomorrow, is there?

EVELYN I guess that he and the authorities see a different tomorrow.

THEMBI Is he ever coming back home?

EVELYN Dear Nelson. Thembi misses you. Terribly. The other day he went into the bedroom. He saw one of your old suit jackets and he put it on. It hung on him but he would not let me take it off. He talks less.

NELSON African women wanted to be with their menfolk and not be permanently widowed in the Reserves. Africans wanted to be allowed out at eleven o'clock at night and not to be confined to their rooms like little children. Africans wanted to be allowed to travel in their own country, and to seek work where they wanted to and not where they were told they had to.

EVELYN I wish you all the best and trust that the court shows you some mercy. We all know that your heart is in the right place. Love Evelyn.

  The CHORUS enters with signs.

NELSON Under the tightest of security we were taken to the Palace of Justice to stand trial. I fully expected to die.

VOICE Mr. Mandela. Your closing remarks.

  BUTI 2 appears in his Xhosian Battle Regalia. A song erupts. The people crowd around BUTI 2.

NELSON Amandla.

CHORUS Ngawethu.

NELSON Amandla.

CHORUS Ngawethu.

POLICEMAN Silence in the court.

BUTI 2 During my lifetime I have dedicated myself to this struggle of the African people. I have fought against White domination and I fought against Black domination. I have cherished the ideal of a democratic and free society in which all persons live together in harmony and with equal opportunities. It is an ideal which I hope to live for and to achieve.

  THEMBI turns off the radio.

But if needs be. It's an ideal for which I am prepared…

NELSON …to die. Like many men before me.

JUDGE Nelson Mandela. Sentence will be passed.

ALL Siyolo
Xoxo
Stowkwe
Tembu
Ndlambe.
Ngqika
Hintsa.
Gadla Henry

King Jongintaba

NELSON   I wasn't going live and be treated as nothing, and to die in the service of a cause would have given my life real meaning. In my deepest heart I wondered if the Elder who had spoken at my manhood ceremony had reached to the house of the great God Qamata. I wondered if he had entered the God's chamber where he lay sleeping, and I wondered if he had kicked him awake. If he had failed, then I knew I was going to die. If he succeeded, then I expected to live.

BUTI 2   Will my name be added to the list of warriors and kings?

NELSON   Qamata are you awake? Elder did you kick him, or will I have to kick our God awake myself?

VOICE   You have been sentenced to life imprisonment on Robben Island.

CHORUS   Amandla. Ngawethu.

NELSON   Life imprisonment. I had lived. There was still hope.

A huge eruption of joy fills the house. BUTI 2 and WALTER are bound together. The CHORUS dances with them. The song continues. The lights shift. The voices of the CHORUS fade until there is only the voices of NELSON and WALTER. Silence. The sound of the ocean. They both look around. GUARD enters.

Robben Island. Political prisoners have been banished to this island for generations.

GUARD   This is your cell, Mandela.

Silence. NELSON watches BUTI 2 enter his cell. He raises his voice in song as he enters. He waits for a response. He gets none.

Welcome to your new home.

NELSON   I was alive. There was still hope.

A male voice begins to sing. Another joins and another joins until they are all singing.

The Island was a wasteland.

GUARD	Wake up.
NELSON	We rose at six each morning. We were given one bowl of water, which we used to shave in and to wash hands and face.
GUARD	Fall in.

BUTI 2 picks up his bowl. He carries it along with the other men to a spot where it is dumped.

NELSON	Each morning we had a few minutes of quiet to talk with other prisoners.

The men greet each other. A quiet song.

GUARD	Fall in.
NELSON	We were served breakfast out of barrels rolled outside.
GUARD	Fall in.
NELSON	And for the next few years we worked, reducing a limestone mountain to rubble.

The men all gather. They begin to work and sing together.

GUARD	Lunch.
NELSON	Work.
GUARD	Dinner.
NELSON	This schedule was adhered to daily.
GUARD	Wake up. Breakfast. Fall in. Lunch. Fall in. Dinner. Bedtime.
NELSON	Each day for years it was the same. Prison, this prison in particular, was created to destroy your spirit. We knew that going in. The routine kept you busy and let you almost forget the world that was still living outside the walls. The whole experience was made easier since so many of my friends were here with me. Together we brought the same energy to keeping our hope breathing as we did to the struggle. We formed discussion groups. We debated ideas. We created life

in this place of death and that helped us forget the
life we had lost. But there were times when you
understood full well where you were. They never let
you forget it.

BUTI 2   I would like something to read. Some books.

GUARD   What?

BUTI 2   Some books. I would like some books to read.

GUARD   Would you?

BUTI 2   Yes.

GUARD   Come with me.

BUTI 2   Where are we going?

GUARD   The library.

NELSON   You were put in solitary confinement for the least
infraction. Just for asking for something to read, you
were locked away for months. But every time I was
let out I asked again. I spent more time in solitary
confinement than I did with the other prisoners. But
we got our books in the end.

Lights up on BUTI 2. He is in his cell reading a book.

I dreamed of going home. Seeing my children.
I dreamed of home of being a child again. Running
through the fields of my home. Free as a bird. Thembi
was now a man. My daughter was a teenager.

GUARD   Mandela you have a visitor.

*NOSEKENI enters. She is aged. BUTI 2 runs to her.
NOSEKENI raises her arms.*

POLICEMAN   You know the rules.

The two of them halt.

BUTI 2   Mother.

NOSEKENI   I had to come and see you…

BUTI 2   You've lost weight.

NOSEKENI	Not from lack of eating.
BUTI 2	Are you feeling all right?
NOSEKENI	There is nothing that you can do for me.
BUTI 2	But we can get you a good doctor.... The children?
NOSEKENI	All of them are well.
BUTI 2	I'm so sorry.
NOSEKENI	For what Buti?
BUTI 2	A son is supposed to look after his mother. Father made sure that I could look after you and... I failed you.
NOSEKENI	Do you remember that story about the young girl with no arms kneeling down to get a drink of water?
BUTI 2	The large bird rose up out of the water... I remember...
NOSEKENI	The bird spoke to the young woman who was so full of shame. The bird, this ancestor, assured the girl that she had committed no crime. She did not deserve the abuse and ill treatment given to her by her father. She was innocent.
NELSON	The girl was engulfed in the wings of the great bird.
NOSEKENI	You remember...
NELSON	That's all that I remember.
NOSEKENI	What happened to her, will happen to you.
NELSON	She died there by the water?
NOSEKENI	No. The bird is the spirit of the ancestors. When she emerged from the spirit's embrace she was whole again. You say that you have failed your father and you failed me, but when I look at you, my son, I see your father. You have done nothing that he would not approve of.
GUARD	Time.
BUTI 2	Let me hug her.

GUARD	Rules Mandela.
BUTI 2	Please. Just a touch. One little…
NOSEKENI	We have touched each other in places that no one sees, my child. You feel me in your heart?
BUTI 2	Deeply.
NOSEKENI	Then I am satisfied. The girl with no arms emerged from the birds embrace, whole. Her arms were back. She held her child in her arms for the very first time. Imagine that. Imagine it.

Lights fade on NOSEKENI.

NELSON	That was the last time I saw her. Word came that she had passed away. I begged the officials to let me attend the funeral…
BUTI 2	I will not escape. It's my duty. Please let me bury her it's my…
GUARD	We are not afraid that you will escape. We are afraid that others will kidnap you and take you abroad. Request denied.
NELSON	Dark days.
GUARD	Letter.
NELSON	The days grew darker as the years stretched out before me.
GUARD	Letter, Mandela.
NELSON	Mail was like gold.

BUTI 2 reads the letter. The men start singing. BUTI 2 walks to his cell.

GUARD	Mandela.

BUTI 2 keeps walking.

Get back here.

BUTI 2 keeps walking.

Mandela.

Lights up on THEMBI.

THEMBI	Are you going to come get me to teach me boxing?
BUTI 2	I promise.
THEMBI	You always promise.
BUTI 2	Tomorrow.
THEMBI	Really?
BUTI 2	Tomorrow is ours. Together.

WALTER enters the cell.

WALTER	My brother.
NELSON	I lay for three days.
WALTER	What is it?
NELSON	Stricken beyond my imagination.
WALTER	Tell me.

NELSON gives WALTER the letter.

We regret to inform you that Thembekile Mandela was killed in a car accident. Nelson.

NELSON	Dark days. Dismal days. Blackness.
THEMBI	Tomorrow, Father. Tomorrow is ours.
BUTI 2	I wanted to be a good son and good father. It's all I wanted. Peace.
WALTER	You have to come outside sometime. The fight is far from over.
NELSON	The years grew longer.

WALTER exits. BUTI 2 reaches into the white soil and rubs his hair with it.

BUTI 2	Qamata. Qamata. Wake up. Wake up.

Lights shift.

Are you asleep?

Lights shift. NOSEKENI reenters. She has changed her costume.

NOSEKENI   Qamata is awake. The ancestors got there before you. What did I always tell you. The ancestors always provide.

BUTI 2 sits on the bed. NOSEKENI puts her arms around him. Lights shift.

NELSON   I sat in prison a forgotten man. Toiling. Reading. Hoping. But as time passed, my name which had fallen from the lips of my people was heard once again in the streets. A new fight emerged and people all over the world began to demand that this whole world of apartheid be destroyed.

The CHORUS enters and begins to sing.

At first it was a lone voice. But over time, more and more voices were added to the chorus.

GUARD   Mandela. The Head of the Prison would like to see you.

NELSON   As the chorus of protest grew I was asked to meet with government officials over my release. Dare I dream? Dare I hope?

GUARD   Mandela?

BUTI 2   Yes.

GUARD   You are being transferred.

BUTI 2 rises.

Mr. Mandela.

BUTI 2   Yes?

NELSON   And finally. After twenty-seven years. There was light.

GUARD   You are free.

Song of celebration. "Free Nelson Mandela" by Jerry Dammers of The Specials. The prison bars rise. The CHORUS dances and sings. Exaltation.

BUTI 2   I have to get my…

GUARD   You are packed. I will take your things out to the car for you.

BUTI 2   You will?

GUARD   Yes, sir.

NELSON   Sir. This was a whole new world for me.

The lights reveal WOMAN 1 holding a baby.

WOMAN 1   Father.

BUTI 2   Is this my little girl?

WOMAN 1   Not anymore.

BUTI 2   Who is this?

WOMAN 1   He is your grandson.

BUTI 2 opens his arms. WOMAN 1 runs into them and hands baby to NELSON. Lights out on BUTI 2.

NELSON   I was an old man. Twenty-seven years. How the world had changed.

POLICEMAN enters.

POLICEMAN   You will have to hurry, sir. I don't know how long we can keep the crowd at bay.

NELSON   I forgot my glasses.

GUARD   I have some here Mr. Mandela.

NELSON   You will need them…

GUARD   I'd be honoured for you to use them.

NELSON   That is very kind of you Mr. Gregory.

GUARD   The country is waiting for you.

GUARD gives NELSON his glasses.

WALTER   The votes are in. The ANC, a formerly outlawed political organisation, has swept into office with a clear majority.

WOMAN 1	Father, are you coming home?
	NELSON gives baby to WOMAN 1.
NELSON	Tomorrow.
	Lights fade on WOMAN 1.
	Today, all of us do, by our presence here… confer glory and hope to newborn liberty. [1]
	NOSEKENI starts to sing the South African National Anthem. It is picked up as it was in Act 1. THEMBI should be the second to join the singing.
	Out of the experience of an extraordinary human disaster, that lasted too long, must be born a society of which all humanity will be proud. We who were outlaws not so long ago have been given the rare privilege to be host of the nations of the world on our own soil. We have at last achieved our political emancipation. Never, never, and never again shall it be that this beautiful land will again experience the oppression of one by another. The sun shall never set on so glorious a human achievement. Let freedom reign. Long live Africa. Amandla.
CHORUS	Ngawethu.
NELSON	Amadla.
CHORUS	Ngawethu.
	The CHORUS freezes in the pose of celebration.
NELSON	All I really ever wanted was to feel like a child again. To feel that I could run to the distant horizon unfettered. That I belonged to the wind, air, water, and mountains and they belonged to me. I was theirs and they were mine. I wanted to have a future and a past. I wanted to believe that the freedom I saw in my dreams was indeed going to be my reality. That I could by dint of hard work, commitment, and

---

[1] Certain phrases in this speech are taken from Mandela's Inaugural Speech, given on May 10, 1994.

imagination, achieve what I saw in my mind's eye.
My dreams were at first selfish and were built to come
true for just me and my family. But over time my
dreams became the dreams for the Xhosa, then all
of Black South Africans, and now they are dreams for
us all. So here I stand, like I always dreamed, out of
prison, free. I stand at the top of the mountain. But
what do I see? More mountains. So join me in making
this dream of freedom for my nation a reality for this
world. My work, your work, our work, is not complete.

The final stanzas of a song.

The end.

Born in Germany, raised in the U.S. and living in Canada for more than twenty years, **Michael A. Miller** is a playwright who has created a diverse range of plays for audiences of all ages. Michael has been the playwright in Residence at both Factory Theatre and Lorraine Kimsa Theatre for Young People. For two seasons he was the coordinator of the CrossCurrents Festival whose mission was to bring works by writers of colour to the Mainstage. He has been the Artistic Director of Theatre Fountainhead, Administrator for Obsidian Theatre Company that, under his direction, produced the highly acclaimed premiere of *The Adventures of A Black Girl in Search of God*. He was also the Artistic Producer of Theatre Fountainhead and Administrator for LKTYP. Most recently he was the Artistic Director of Omiala, A Festival of New Black Culture at Harbourfront. He has extensive experience in Arts and Education where he developed a long-running program for the Toronto District School Board, The Co-op Theatre Company. This program provided professional training opportunities for young people interested in pursuing theatre as a career. As the resident playwright/director at the TDSB he produced ten new original plays for young people that toured across the city to thousands of the children annually and served as a model of new and innovative approaches to arts for young people. Michael has been the recipient of numerous grants from The Canada Council for the Arts, the Toronto Arts Council, and the Ontario Arts Council. He has sat on juries for both the Ontario Arts Council, and the Toronto Arts Council. He has won the prestigious Chalmers Award for excellence in playwriting, and been nominated for outstanding work by the Writers Guild of Great Britain. In 2004 he was selected as one of the twelve outstanding artists to be featured on the OAC's fortieth anniversary website.